Fun Fan Facts:
The Unofficial NBA Edition

Sacramento Kings

Everything Young Sacramento Kings Fans Should Know

By: Jake Liam

Dedication

To every Kings fan who has shown up, season after season, through the rebuilds, the close calls, and the loud nights at Golden 1 Center. Sacramento is a basketball city, and this book is proof of it.

This one is for the 916.

THE NBA BY THE NUMBERS

MOST NBA CHAMPIONSHIPS*

- CELTICS (18) †
- LAKERS (17)
- WARRIORS (7)
- BULLS (6)
- SPURS (5)

*As of the 2024-25 Season. † One Trophy = 4 Championships.

NBA HISTORY SNAPSHOT

1946 — NBA Founded
1954 — Shot Clock Introduced
1979 — 3-Point Line Added
2023 — NBA Cup Introduced

BIG NUMBERS

$156 million
Stephen Curry's est. earnings in the 24-25 season

7'7"
Tallest player in NBA history (Gheorghe Mureşan & Manute Bol)

30 | 4 | 82

30 — Teams Competing in the NBA
4 — Playoff Rounds
82 — Games Per Season

SACRAMENTO KINGS
IN THE NBA

- FOUNDED: 1945 †
- NBA TITLES: 1
- CONFERENCE TITLES: 1*

36 Playoff Appearances

† Founding dates are complicated & may cause arguments at Thanksgiving. Ask someone born before color TV. All Titles reflect pre-relocation franchise history. * As of 2024-25 Season.

NBA ALL-TIME MVP LEADERS

KAREEM ABDUL-JABBAR (6) ★ MICHAEL JORDAN (5) ★ BILL RUSSELL (5)

EASTERN CONFERENCE

Atlantic – **Celtics**
Atlantic – **Nets**
Atlantic – **Knicks**
Atlantic – **76ers**
Atlantic – **Raptors**
Central – **Bulls**
Central – **Cavaliers**
Central – **Pistons**
Central – **Pacers**
Central – **Bucks**
Southeast – **Hawks**
Southeast – **Hornets**
Southeast – **Heat**
Southeast – **Magic**
Southeast – **Wizards**

WESTERN CONFERENCE

Pacific – **Lakers**
Pacific – **Clippers**
Pacific – **Warriors**
Pacific – **Suns**
Pacific – **Kings**
Northwest – **Nuggets**
Northwest – **Timberwolves**
Northwest – **Thunder**
Northwest – **Trail Blazers**
Northwest – **Jazz**
Southwest – **Mavericks**
Southwest – **Rockets**
Southwest – **Spurs**
Southwest – **Pelicans**
Southwest – **Grizzlies**

Introduction

Welcome, fans! Whether you're new to cheering for the Sacramento Kings or you've been bleeding the team colors your whole life, this book is packed with fun, exciting facts about your favorite team. Get ready to impress your friends and family with everything you know about the Sacramento Kings.

Quick Timeout

This book is packed with stats. Like, A LOT of stats. Every fact was checked, double-checked, and triple-checked. But here's the thing about basketball history: not everyone agrees on everything. Ask someone who watched games before color TV and someone who grew up with instant replay and you'll get two completely different answers. My dad, stepdad, uncle, and grandpa all argued about the same fact. Four people. Four answers. All of them think they're right. So if you spot something that doesn't match what you've heard, congratulations. You might be a bigger fan than the people who helped make this book. And honestly? That's pretty cool.

HOW IT WORKS

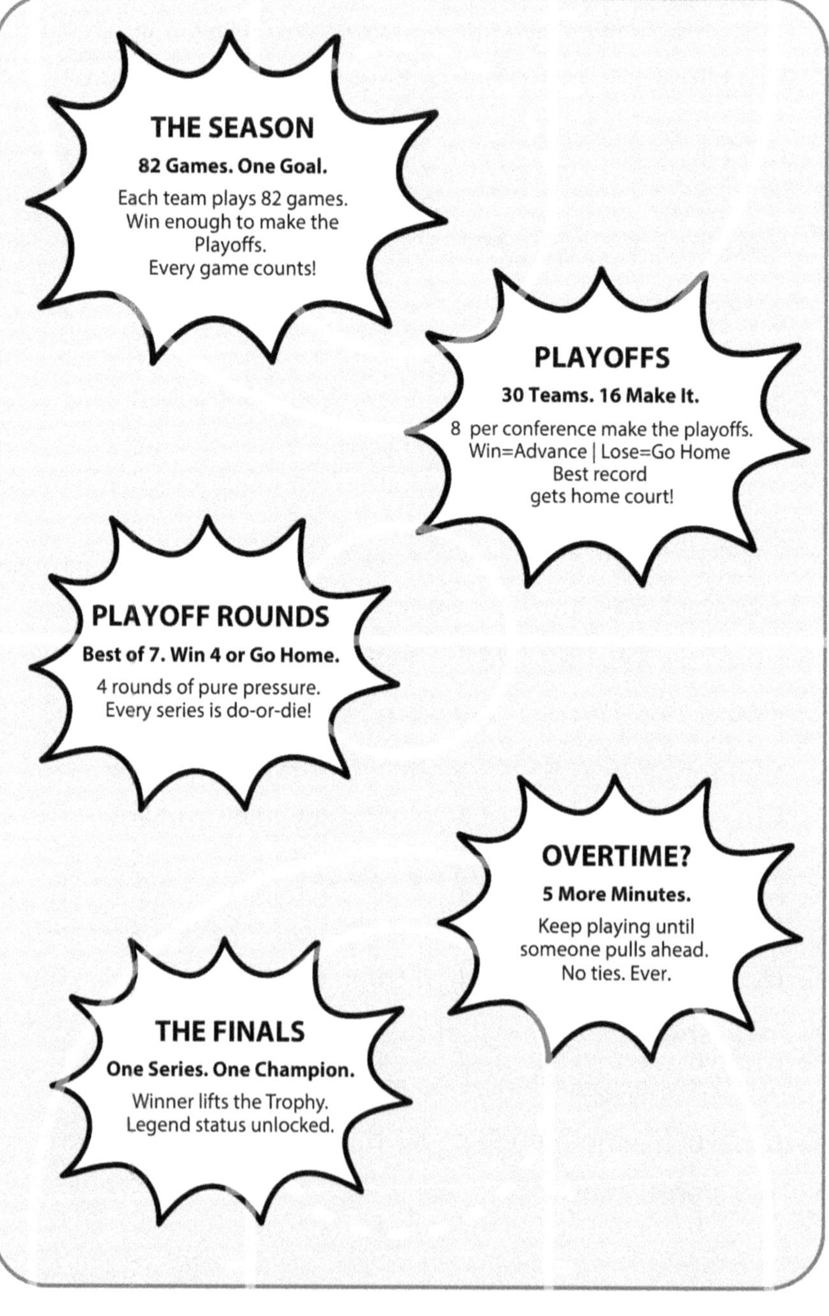

THE SEASON
82 Games. One Goal.
Each team plays 82 games.
Win enough to make the
Playoffs.
Every game counts!

PLAYOFFS
30 Teams. 16 Make It.
8 per conference make the playoffs.
Win=Advance | Lose=Go Home
Best record
gets home court!

PLAYOFF ROUNDS
Best of 7. Win 4 or Go Home.
4 rounds of pure pressure.
Every series is do-or-die!

OVERTIME?
5 More Minutes.
Keep playing until
someone pulls ahead.
No ties. Ever.

THE FINALS
One Series. One Champion.
Winner lifts the Trophy.
Legend status unlocked.

How the NBA Works

At first glance, basketball feels simple. Ten players. One ball. Two hoops. Go.

Then the NBA adds the layers.

An 82-game regular season. A draft where bad teams pick first. Playoffs that last two full months. Superstars who can change everything with one trade. Dynasties that rise, fall, and rise again.

And somehow, it all works.

The NBA is built on one big idea: every team gets a chance to reset, reload, and rise again. No relegation. No dropping down to a lower league. Just basketball, every night, from October through June.

It is a league designed for drama, stars, and comebacks. And once you understand the flow, it is impossible to stop watching.

The League Setup

The NBA has 30 teams, spread across the United States and Canada. Those teams are split into two conferences:

- Eastern Conference
- Western Conference

Each conference has three divisions, mostly based on geography. Divisions matter for scheduling, but not as much as they used to.

Every team plays 82 regular season games, usually from October through April. Home games. Road games. Back-to-back nights. Long road trips. The season is a marathon before the sprint even starts.

Win games, and you climb the standings. Lose too many, and the pressure builds fast.

How Games Are Played

An NBA game has four quarters, each lasting 12 minutes. That means 48 minutes of game time, plus timeouts, free throws, and the occasional coach argument that adds another 20 minutes nobody planned for.

Scoring is simple:

- A shot inside the three-point line is worth 2 points
- A shot beyond the arc is worth 3 points
- Free throws are worth 1 point

If the score is tied at the end of regulation, the game goes to overtime, which lasts 5 minutes. Still tied? Another overtime. Keep going until someone wins.

There is a shot clock too. Teams have 24 seconds to take a shot. No standing around. No holding the ball forever. Keep it moving.

The Regular Season Race

The regular season is long for a reason. It tests everything.

Depth. Health. Focus. Patience.

Teams play opponents from both conferences, but they face conference rivals more often. By the end of the season, each conference's top teams have earned their playoff spots the hard way.

The goal is simple: make the playoffs. But there is a twist.

The NBA Cup

In 2023, the NBA added something new to the middle of the season. Something with actual stakes. They called it the In-Season Tournament, now known as the NBA Cup.

It works like this: Every team plays a small group stage during November and December, with special court designs that look like nothing else in basketball. The best teams advance to a knockout round held in Las Vegas.

The winners split a prize pool. Players earn bonus money. And for the first time, a team could lift a trophy before the playoffs even started.

Some fans are still warming up to it. Some players love it. But the moment a team starts treating it seriously and a crowd shows up buzzing in December, it feels like something.

Which, honestly, sounds about right.

The Play-In Tournament

Instead of sending the top eight teams from each conference straight to the playoffs, the NBA added something new. The Play-In Tournament.

Here is how it works:

- Teams ranked 1 through 6 in each conference are safe
- Teams ranked 7 through 10 fight for the final two playoff spots

The 7 and 8 seeds have an advantage. Win once and you are in. Lose and you still get one more shot. The 9 and 10 seeds have to win twice in a row just to earn a first-round matchup.

It turns the end of the season into a sprint. Every game suddenly matters more. Fans love it. Coaches age rapidly.

The NBA Playoffs

Once the playoffs begin, everything tightens.

Sixteen teams enter. Eight from each conference. Every round is a best-of-seven games series. That means the first team to win four games moves on:

- First Round
- Conference Semifinals
- Conference Finals
- NBA Finals

Home-court advantage matters. Crowds get louder. Rotations get shorter. Superstars play heavier minutes. One bad quarter can flip a series. One great performance can define a career.

By the time the NBA Finals arrive in June, only two teams are left. One from the East. One from the West. Four wins away from a championship. Four wins away from history.

The NBA Draft: Hope Begins Here

Here is where the NBA gets clever. Every summer, new players enter the league through the NBA Draft. Teams take turns selecting college players, international stars, and teenagers straight out of high school.

The teams that finished with the worst records get the best odds to pick early through the Draft Lottery. It is not guaranteed, but it gives struggling franchises a real shot at changing their future with one pick.

That means one bad season does not doom you forever. It might actually change everything. Some franchises are rebuilt by a single draft night moment.

Hope shows up wearing a new jersey.

No Relegation. All Pressure.

Unlike many global sports leagues, NBA teams never drop down to a lower league. They always stay in the NBA.

That does not mean there is no pressure.

Fans remember losing seasons. Owners make changes. Coaches get replaced. Players get traded. Every year is a test of direction, patience, and belief.

Stars, Systems, and Showtime

The NBA is famous for its stars. But stars do not win alone.

Teams need chemistry. Coaches need systems. Role players need to deliver on the biggest stages. One injury. One hot streak. One trade deadline deal. Any of it can flip a season.

That balance between individual brilliance and team basketball is what makes the league special.

Fast breaks. Buzzer-beaters. Game 7s. And moments that get replayed forever. That is the NBA.

Once you get the flow, it is pure electricity.

Sacramento Kings Facts

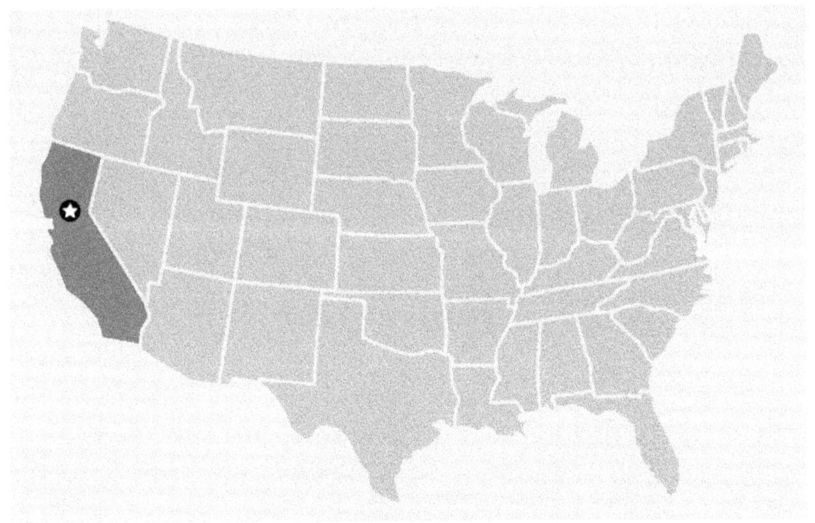

Home City

Sacramento, California

Metro Area Population

About 2.5 Million

Home Arena

Golden 1 Center

Arena Capacity

17,608

Conference / Division

Western Conference / Pacific Division

Famous Local Food

Farm-to-fork cuisine, avocado, NorCal burritos, almond everything

Chapter 1: From Cincinnati to Sacramento

1. A Team With More Addresses Than a Fugitive

Most NBA franchises pick a city and stay there. The Sacramento Kings looked at that idea and said, "Nah, let's try a few." Before they ever set foot in California, this team lived two completely different lives in two completely different states, and honestly, their journey to Sacramento reads less like a sports history and more like a road trip that kept going wrong.

The franchise started in 1945 as the Rochester Royals, playing in upstate New York during the era when basketball was still figuring out what it wanted to be. They won an NBA championship in 1951, which is great, except almost nobody today connects that trophy to Sacramento because the team was literally called the Royals and playing in Rochester at the time. Then came Cincinnati in 1957, then Kansas City in 1972, where they became the Kings. By the time Sacramento entered the picture in 1985, this franchise had been around for forty years and still had not found a permanent home.

That is a lot of moving boxes for one basketball team. Most people move once or twice in a lifetime and consider it traumatic. This team did it three times before landing in a city that finally, truly, completely lost its mind over them. Sometimes it just takes a while to find your people.

2. The Underdog City That Refused to Lose

Sacramento should not have gotten an NBA team. At least, that was the opinion of basically everyone who was not from Sacramento. When the Kansas City Kings became available in the mid-1980s, several cities made pitches, and Sacramento was considered the longest of long shots. It was smaller than most NBA markets, not exactly on the radar of league executives, and did not have an arena that met NBA standards. On paper, it made no sense.

What Sacramento had instead was something that could not be written in a spreadsheet: pure, unhinged, overwhelming enthusiasm. Local businessman Gregg Lukenbill and a group of investors put together a bid that included a promise to build a new arena fast, and the city backed them up with a level of community energy that genuinely surprised the NBA. A fan vote in Sacramento drew enormous support. People showed up. People cared. People acted like their entire identity was on the line, which, for a mid-sized California city that had never had a major professional sports team, it kind of was.

The NBA approved the move in 1985, and Sacramento became one of the smallest markets in the league to host an NBA franchise. Every other city that got passed over probably did a lot of grumbling. Sacramento did a lot of celebrating. Turns out, wanting something badly enough actually works sometimes. Who knew.

3. Year One: Loud, Chaotic, and Completely Sold Out

Imagine this: it is November 1985, the Kings have just arrived in Sacramento, and the city has never seen anything like this before. Not because the team was good. They were not particularly good. But because the building was absolutely electric every single night, filled with fans who were still pinching themselves that this was actually happening.

The Kings went 37 and 45 in their first Sacramento season, which is a polite way of saying they lost a lot. Their best player that year was Reggie Theus, a smooth guard with style to spare, but the roster was still finding its footing in a brand new city. None of that mattered to the fans. ARCO Arena, the temporary facility they played in that first year, was loud in a way that surprised visiting teams who had maybe not put Sacramento on their list of hostile road environments.

Season ticket sales were a phenomenon. The Kings sold out games consistently in that first year, which sent a message to the entire league that this market was real. Other NBA cities with longer histories and bigger reputations sometimes struggled to fill seats. Sacramento, in year one, with a sub-.500 team, was packing the house. The city had waited a long time for this. They were not about to waste it sitting quietly.

4. The Madhouse on Market Street: Sacramento's Glorious Warehouse Arena

When Sacramento promised the NBA an arena in 1985, they delivered one the way a student delivers a paper the morning it is due: fast, functional, and held together with more determination than anyone would like to admit. The original ARCO Arena was a converted 82,000 square foot warehouse that cost somewhere between seven and twelve million dollars to build, which for context is less than many current NBA players spend on cars. It was the smallest arena in the league at the time, holding exactly 10,333 people, and it was so obviously temporary that everyone involved acknowledged it out loud and simply did not care. Sacramento had a team. The team had a building. Details could be sorted later.

The details were extraordinary. Visiting teams could not dress at the arena because the locker rooms were roughly the size of a standard hotel room, so opposing NBA players were bused in from their hotels in their uniforms like they were on a field trip. There were four suites in the entire building, one in each corner, which is four fewer suites than most modern arenas have in a single hallway. The farthest seat from the court was 120 feet away, meaning the crowd was so close to the action that players could hear individual conversations from the stands, which sounds charming until you consider what those conversations probably contained.

The first event ever held at the original ARCO Arena was a fashion show, which is either the most Sacramento thing imaginable or proof that the building had absolutely no idea what it was about to become. The first Kings game there ended in a loss to the Los Angeles Clippers, which set a tone the franchise would spend the next several decades trying to correct. The building also held the distinction of being one of the first arenas in NBA history to sell naming rights, which means Sacramento inadvertently invented something that every sports venue in the world now does. The original structure still exists today as a California government office building on North Market Boulevard, looking almost identical on the outside to how it looked during Kings games, quietly housing state bureaucrats where NBA basketball once happened. Somewhere nearby, the ghost of a warehouse that became a legend is extremely proud of itself.

5. ARCO to Golden 1: An Arena Glow-Up Decades in the Making

After three seasons in the converted warehouse, the Kings moved two miles north in 1988 into a proper permanent arena, still called ARCO Arena, still surrounded by farmland, and still selling out consistently. This version held 17,317 people, cost forty million dollars to build, which was actually the lowest construction cost of any NBA arena at the time, and immediately developed a home court advantage that visiting teams genuinely dreaded. It was not fancy. It was not cutting edge. What it was, was loud in a way that newer and shinier buildings spent decades trying to replicate and usually could not.

The arena went through an identity crisis in its later years that mirrored the franchise's own turbulence. When ARCO's naming rights expired in 2011, the building was briefly renamed Power Balance Pavilion, after a company that sold rubber wristbands that claimed to improve athletic performance and were later found to do absolutely nothing. Then it became Sleep Train Arena in 2013, named after a mattress company, which is a sentence that exists in real history. Through all of it, the building remained standing while ownership drama swirled around it and relocation threats came and went, with Sacramento fighting off a Seattle bid in 2013 to keep the Kings in California.

Golden 1 Center opened in downtown Sacramento in October 2016 and immediately rendered all previous arenas irrelevant by comparison. The full story of what Golden 1 Center meant for Sacramento gets its proper treatment in Chapter 3. For now, just know this: cowbells sound even better in there, and visiting teams are still not happy about it.

6. Oscar Robertson: The Big O (1960-1970)

Before we get into the Sacramento Kings era specifically, we need to talk about Oscar Robertson, because leaving him out of this franchise's story would be like writing about the history of pizza and skipping the part where someone invented dough. Robertson played for the Cincinnati Royals from 1960 to 1970, back when this franchise was still decades away from California, and what he did during that time was so absurd it still makes modern NBA players uncomfortable to think about too hard.

In the 1961-62 season, Oscar Robertson averaged a triple-double for the entire year. Points, rebounds, and assists. All three categories. All season long. This was not a hot streak. This was not a good month. This was 79 games of being so comprehensively good at basketball that the sport essentially had to invent a new way to measure greatness just to explain him. When modern players post a triple-double in a single game, reporters make a big deal about it. Robertson did it on average. Every game. For a year.

He was so far ahead of his time that the NBA did not even fully appreciate what it was watching. Robertson was a point guard who could score, pass, rebound, defend, and probably reorganize your sock drawer if you asked nicely. The Cincinnati Royals never won a championship with him, which is one of the great injustices in basketball history. The man deserved better. He got a statue and a legacy instead, which is nice, but still.

Oscar Robertson rises for a short jumper while three Knicks defenders try their luck. Spoiler: good luck with that. "The Big O" starred for the Cincinnati Royals, the franchise that later became today's Sacramento Kings. Robertson was so good he averaged a triple-double for an entire NBA season. Points, rebounds, assists. All of them. All the time. *Photo: Oscar Robertson of the Cincinnati Royals vs the New York Knicks. Photograph via Wikimedia Commons. Public domain. Source: Wikimedia Commons.*

7. Mitch Richmond: Rock (1991-1998)

Mitch Richmond was a six-time NBA All-Star, an Olympic gold medalist, a Hall of Famer, and one of the most unstoppable scorers of the 1990s. He also played most of his prime years in Sacramento, which is part of why a concerning number of people have absolutely no idea who he is. This is not an exaggeration. Ask a casual basketball fan to name a famous Sacramento King and they will say Chris Webber. Mitch Richmond, who was quietly doing everything short of performing miracles for nearly a decade in purple and gold, tends to get a polite blank stare followed by a subject change.

Richmond arrived in Sacramento in 1991 after being traded from Golden State, and he immediately became the face of the franchise. He could score from anywhere, create his own shot in a way that made defenders look like they were moving in slow motion, and he did it all on teams that were constantly rebuilding and shuffling rosters around him. Richmond averaged over 21 points per game for Sacramento. He made six All-Star teams as a King. He won the All-Star Game MVP in 1995. He was legitimately one of the best players in the entire NBA for the better part of a decade.

And yet. Here we are. If basketball history were a group project, Mitch Richmond would be the teammate who did half the work and still did not get his name on the poster. The Hall of Fame corrected this injustice in 2014. Sacramento always knew. The rest of the world is still catching up, and that is honestly their problem.

8. Chris Webber and Vlade Divac: C-Webb and the Flopper (1998-2004)

The late 1990s and early 2000s Kings were built around two players who could not have been more different and somehow made it work perfectly. Chris Webber was a 6-foot-10 power forward who could dribble like a guard, pass like a point guard, and score like someone who had never once heard the word "defender." Vlade Divac was a 7-foot Serbian center with the passing instincts of a wizard and a talent for drawing fouls that bordered on professional theater. Together they made Sacramento one of the most exciting teams in the league and gave Kings fans a stretch of basketball they still talk about with the kind of reverence usually reserved for family heirlooms.

Webber arrived via trade in 1998 and transformed the Kings almost immediately. He was the kind of player who made everything around him better, partly through talent and partly through sheer force of personality. Sacramento went from a lottery team to a legitimate title contender in what felt like about fifteen minutes. Vlade, meanwhile, was already beloved in Sacramento for his passing and his personality, and the two formed a frontcourt that opposing defenses genuinely had no good answer for.

Now, Vlade Divac was also one of the great floppers in NBA history, and it would be a real disservice to skip over this. The man could hit the floor at the slightest contact with the grace and commitment of a Broadway actor who had been waiting his entire life for this specific moment. Referees called it. Opponents screamed about it. Vlade would get up, smile warmly, and do it again on the very next possession. It was absolutely infuriating if you were rooting against him. If you were a Kings fan, it was basically a free entertainment bonus on top of an already great team.

9. Peja Stojakovic: The Human Laser (1998-2006)

Peja Stojakovic was not built like your typical NBA star. He was long and a little wiry, not the most explosive athlete in the league, and he did not make highlight reels with dunks or crossovers. What Peja did was shoot the basketball with a level of precision that made it seem like the laws of physics had personally agreed to do him a favor. The ball would leave his hands at a trajectory that looked slightly too perfect, arc through the air like it had somewhere important to be, and drop through the net with a swish so clean it almost sounded polite.

Stojakovic came to Sacramento from Europe, where he had already established himself as one of the best players on the continent, and he became a critical piece of those early 2000s Kings teams that nearly won a championship. He led the NBA in three-point percentage during some of his best seasons and won the Three-Point Shootout at All-Star Weekend twice, which is the basketball equivalent of winning a hot dog eating contest and then coming back the next year purely out of principle.

What made Peja genuinely dangerous was that he barely needed any space. A half-step of separation was enough. A quick catch and release and the ball was already gone before the defender processed what had happened. Opposing coaches drew up entire defensive game plans specifically designed to keep the ball out of his hands. Sometimes it worked. Mostly it did not. The net swished politely either way, as if apologizing to everyone involved.

10. De'Aaron Fox: Swipa (2017-Present)

De'Aaron Fox might be the fastest player in the NBA. This is not casual praise. This is a conclusion that coaches, analysts, and defenders who have spent several years watching him vanish into the paint have arrived at with genuine resignation. Fox in transition is essentially a cheat code that the rest of the league has not figured out how to patch. By the time a defense gets set, he is already past them, already at the rim, already making the decision that ends the possession. It happens quickly. Embarrassingly quickly. The kind of quickly where you blink and then have to check the scoreboard to confirm what you think just happened actually happened.

Fox was drafted fifth overall by Sacramento in 2017 and took a few seasons to become the player the Kings believed he would be. When it finally clicked, it clicked loudly. He developed into one of the premier point guards in the Western Conference, a player capable of dropping 30 points while also running the offense, locking up on defense, and making teammates around him better. In 2023, he led Sacramento to the playoffs for the first time in sixteen years, ending the longest active drought in North American professional sports. Some Kings fans had literally been born, grown up, graduated high school, and started full-time jobs in the time between playoff appearances.

Fox's nickname is Swipa, as in Swiper from Dora the Explorer, because he swipes the ball. It is a nickname that started as a joke and stuck permanently, which is very on-brand for a player whose entire career has involved doing things faster than anyone expects. His first step is so quick that defenders occasionally just watch it happen the way you watch a magic trick, knowing something is being done to you and being completely unable to stop it. Sacramento built their entire identity around him. When you have something that fast, you do not ask it to slow down.

11. The 2002 Western Conference Finals: The Series That Still Hurts

The 2002 Western Conference Finals between the Sacramento Kings and the Los Angeles Lakers is one of the greatest playoff series in NBA history, and if you are a Kings fan, that sentence is both a compliment and a wound that never fully healed. Sacramento came into that series as a legitimate contender, armed with Chris Webber, Vlade Divac, Peja Stojakovic, Mike Bibby, and one of the most gifted offensive rosters the Western Conference had seen in years. They were not underdogs. They were genuinely supposed to win this thing.

And for a while, they were doing exactly that. The Kings pushed the defending champion Lakers to seven games, trading wins back and forth in a series so competitive and so intense that even casual fans who had never cared about either team found themselves watching through their fingers. Sacramento won Games 1, 3, and 4. Los Angeles won Games 2 and 5. Heading into Game 6, the Kings led the series three games to two. They were one win away from the NBA Finals. One win away from the biggest moment in franchise history. Everything was set up perfectly.

Then Game 6 happened. We will get to Game 6.

12. Game 6: The Most Controversial Game in NBA History

Game 6 of the 2002 Western Conference Finals is not just famous. It is infamous. It is the kind of game that Sacramento fans can describe in precise detail twenty-plus years later, not because they love the memory but because the human brain has a special filing system for events that were deeply, profoundly unfair. The Kings lost that game 106 to 102. They lost the series in Game 7. And the way Game 6 unfolded left a mark on the entire franchise that never fully faded.

The numbers told the story that words struggled to capture. The Los Angeles Lakers shot 40 free throws in that game. Sacramento shot 25. In the fourth quarter alone, the Lakers went to the line 27 times. For context, 27 free throws in a single quarter is roughly the same number a team might shoot in an entire normal game. Replays showed calls that made no sense. Non-calls that made even less sense. The building in Los Angeles was confused. The broadcast team was confused. Sacramento was furious.

Years later, disgraced referee Tim Donaghy, who was convicted of gambling on NBA games he officiated, alleged that two referees assigned to Game 6 had been directed to extend the series. The NBA investigated and denied the claim. The controversy never fully resolved, which means it never fully went away either. Kings fans did not need Donaghy to tell them something felt wrong that night. They had watched Game 6. They already knew. Some injustices do not require a confession. They just require eyes.

13. The Night Sacramento Almost Lost Everything

In 2013, the Sacramento Kings nearly ceased to exist as a Sacramento entity, and the story of how the city held on is one of the most dramatic ownership battles in professional sports history. The Maloof family, who had owned the Kings since 1998, decided they wanted out of Sacramento. They found a buyer: a Seattle-based ownership group that wanted to bring the team to Washington state and presumably rename it something that had nothing to do with royalty or California. The deal was essentially done. Sacramento was going to lose its team.

What happened next was a full-scale civic mobilization that the NBA genuinely did not see coming. Sacramento mayor Kevin Johnson, a former NBA point guard who understood the league from the inside, flew to New York, met with Commissioner David Stern directly, and put together a competing ownership bid backed by new investors and a concrete arena plan. He used every connection and every piece of credibility he had built both on the court and in politics to make the case that Sacramento deserved to keep its team. The fact that he was a former NBA player meant the league took him seriously in rooms where a regular mayor might have been politely shown the exit.

In May 2013, the NBA Board of Governors voted 22 to 8 to keep the Kings in Sacramento. The city celebrated like they had won a championship, which in a way they had, because the alternative was losing professional basketball entirely. The Seattle group walked away. Sacramento exhaled. Sacramento kept the Kings. Seattle kept waiting. Sometimes the underdog story actually ends correctly.

14. The 2023 Playoffs: Sixteen Years Is a Long Time to Wait

The Sacramento Kings last appeared in the NBA playoffs in 2006. The team that broke that drought in 2023 was built by a front office that had a plan, a fanbase that had been waiting with the patience of people who had completely run out of patience, and a point guard named De'Aaron Fox who was fast enough to make sixteen years of losing feel like a distant memory in about forty games.

The Kings went 48 and 34 in the 2022-23 season, their best record in years, and clinched a playoff spot while the city of Sacramento processed something it had almost forgotten was possible. The celebration when the Kings officially punched their ticket was not subtle.

Golden 1 Center was loud in a way that suggested the building itself had been waiting. Fans who had supported the Kings through the lean years, the draft lottery seasons, the ownership drama, the relocation threats, and the endless rebuilding cycles were suddenly watching playoff basketball again.

Sacramento faced the Golden State Warriors in the first round and pushed them to seven games before losing, which was both heartbreaking and completely on-brand for a fanbase that has historically experienced everything the hard way. But the series itself was electric. Two California teams, one of them a dynasty and one of them finally back where it belonged, going the distance in a series that reminded everyone why the playoffs exist. The drought was over. The cowbells were ringing. Sixteen years is a long time to wait, but Sacramento showed up for every single one of them, which is either deeply admirable or slightly concerning, depending on your perspective.

15. Golden 1 Center: Half a Billion Dollars Well Spent

Golden 1 Center opened on October 4, 2016, cost approximately half a billion dollars to build, sits in the heart of downtown Sacramento, and immediately became one of the finest arenas in the NBA. It was the first indoor arena in North America to be powered entirely by solar energy, which is deeply California of it and also genuinely impressive for anyone who has ever tried to power so much as a reading lamp with a solar panel. The acoustics were designed specifically to maximize crowd noise, which means whoever approved those acoustics either loves Sacramento basketball or actively enjoys watching visiting teams lose their minds.

The difference between Golden 1 Center and the old ARCO Arena is roughly the difference between a private jet and a bus that might or might not show up on time. ARCO was beloved because of the atmosphere its fans created inside it despite everything. Golden 1 took that same atmosphere and gave it a building that finally matched. Downtown Sacramento was transformed. Restaurants opened. Businesses followed. An arena became a neighborhood anchor, which is exactly what the city had been promised and exactly what it delivered.

The Kings' first regular-season game at Golden 1 Center was against the San Antonio Spurs on October 27, 2016, and Sacramento lost 102 to 94. Which, honestly, was very on-brand for a franchise that has rarely done anything the easy way. The cowbells were present, loud, and extremely unhappy to be in an enclosed space with superior acoustics. The Spurs left town with the win. Sacramento kept the building, the energy, and the long game. Visiting teams have confirmed ever since that Golden 1 Center is among the toughest road environments in the league. The arena that Sacramento fought for, nearly lost, and waited years to build turned out to be exactly worth all of it. The Spurs got two points that night. Sacramento got everything else.

16. Slamson the Lion: A Mascot Who Has Absolutely No Chill

Sacramento is called the Kings. Their mascot is a lion. This makes complete sense if you think about it for approximately one second and zero sense if you think about it for any longer than that, because lions are not kings in any basketball-related way, and Sacramento is not particularly known for its lion population. And yet here we are. Slamson the Lion has been the face of Kings game entertainment since 1994 and has committed fully to the bit in a way that deserves genuine respect.

Slamson does not walk onto the court. Slamson arrives. He dunks off trampolines. He rides motorcycles into arenas. He gets shot out of things. He has been involved in more pregame stunts than a reasonable lion mascot probably should be, and he approaches every single one of them with the energy of someone who has had too much coffee and nowhere appropriate to put it. At various points in Kings history, when the team on the floor was not providing much entertainment value, Slamson was essentially carrying the entire franchise's fun quota by himself. He deserves a contract extension and possibly a therapist.

What makes Slamson genuinely great as a mascot is that he leans into the chaos rather than away from it. He taunts opposing players. He messes with referees. He does things that would get an actual person removed from the building and gets away with it because he is technically a lion and therefore operating under a different set of social rules. Every NBA team has a mascot. Very few mascots have a personality. Slamson has more personality than some starting lineups, and the Kings would be significantly less fun without him showing up and ruining someone's evening on a nightly basis.

17. The Cowbell: A Piece of Farm Equipment That Became a Religion

Somewhere in Sacramento's early basketball history, a person made a decision. That decision was to bring a cowbell to an NBA game. There is no record of who this person was, no plaque commemorating the moment, no historical marker on the spot where it happened. And yet that anonymous cowbell carrier inadvertently created one of the most recognizable fan traditions in professional sports, which is either a testament to the unpredictable nature of cultural history or proof that basketball fans will adopt literally anything if you give them enough time.

The cowbell caught on the way good ideas sometimes do, which is to say chaotically and without anyone planning it. One cowbell became several. Several became many. Many became an entire arena full of people clanging metal instruments during a basketball game, creating a noise level that visiting teams have described using words that are not suitable for a book aimed at young readers. The Kings organization eventually leaned into it completely, selling official Kings cowbells at the arena, building marketing campaigns around it, and embracing the fact that their fanbase is identified by a piece of equipment normally used to locate livestock.

The official nickname is Cowbell Kingdom, which sounds like either the greatest theme park ever conceived or a very niche country music festival. It is neither. It is just Sacramento, doing Sacramento things, at volumes that make opposing point guards genuinely struggle to hear their own coaches during timeouts. The actor Christopher Walken once did a famous comedy sketch about needing more cowbell. Sacramento basketball fans said "You know what this Kings game needs? More cowbell." They were right.

18. The Purple and Gold Chronicles: A Jersey History Nobody Asked For But Everyone Needs

The Sacramento Kings have worn purple and gold since arriving in California in 1985, which means they have shared a color scheme with the Los Angeles Lakers for four decades, which means there is a conversation happening somewhere right now between a confused child and a patient parent trying to explain why two California basketball teams look vaguely similar. The Kings have handled this by periodically changing their uniforms enough to stay distinct, though the purple has remained a constant, because once you commit to purple in the NBA, you commit to it forever.

The original Sacramento uniforms were straightforward: purple, gold, white, a crown logo, relatively simple. Over the years the shade of purple shifted, the gold got brighter, the crown got redesigned, and various alternate jerseys arrived with varying degrees of success. In 2014 the Kings unveiled a significant rebrand with a new crown logo and a sharper color palette that was generally well received, which in NBA uniform history counts as a major victory because most rebrands generate approximately equal amounts of love and outrage regardless of how good they actually look.

The Kings also famously wore a black alternate jersey for a period that divided fans cleanly into two camps: people who thought black was a bold and modern choice, and people who thought the Kings should be in purple or they should not be playing basketball at all. Both groups still exist and still feel strongly about this. The purple ultimately won, as it always does, because it is the one color in professional sports that says "yes, we are royalty, and also we are from California, and yes, we know the Lakers exist, and no, we are not talking about it."

19. Farm to Fork: The Kings Play Basketball in a City That Takes Vegetables Very Seriously

Sacramento calls itself the Farm to Fork Capital of America, which is a real official designation and not something a local tourism board made up at a very optimistic afternoon meeting. The Sacramento region produces an extraordinary amount of the food consumed across the United States, from almonds to tomatoes to rice to a variety of other things you have eaten without ever thinking about where they came from. The Kings play basketball in a city that is quietly feeding the country, and they have embraced this identity in ways that are either charming or deeply unexpected depending on how much you expected an NBA franchise to have strong opinions about locally sourced produce.

Golden 1 Center has leaned into the farm to fork identity harder than any NBA arena has any business doing. The concessions feature local Sacramento Valley ingredients. The team has partnered with regional farms and food producers. There are actual thoughtful food options inside a professional sports arena, which if you have ever eaten stadium nachos with a completely broken spirit will understand is a significant upgrade from the norm. The Kings have essentially made good food part of their brand, which is either very California or very smart or, more likely, both at the same time.

The juxtaposition of NBA basketball and artisanal agriculture is genuinely delightful if you let yourself appreciate it. Somewhere in the world right now there is a visiting NBA player eating a locally sourced almond-crusted something at Golden 1 Center and having complicated feelings about it. Sacramento does not care. Sacramento is very proud of its almonds and is not going to apologize for that, not to you, not to anyone, not ever.

20. The Wildest Trades in Kings History: A Support Group Waiting to Happen

The Sacramento Kings have made some trades over the years that required a long sit-down afterward. Not all of them were bad in the moment. Several of them looked completely reasonable when they happened and only revealed their true nature later, the way a suspicious noise in your car gets ignored for three weeks and then becomes a very expensive problem. The Kings' trade history is essentially a masterclass in how NBA roster construction can go wrong, right, and completely sideways within the same five-year window.

The most famous trade in Kings history is one they did
not make rather than one they did. In 2002,
Sacramento was offered Kobe Bryant in a
sign-and-trade deal by the Los Angeles Lakers. The
Kings declined. Kobe Bryant went on to win three more
championships in Los Angeles over the next decade.
Sacramento went on to win zero. This fact lives
rent-free in the head of every Kings fan who knows
about it, which is all of them, because someone always
brings it up, especially around the anniversary of Game
6, which is not a coincidence.

More recently, the Kings traded away draft picks in
quantities that made observers genuinely concerned
about the long-term structural integrity of the
franchise. At one point Sacramento had traded so many
future first-round picks that their draft situation
resembled a game of hot potato where somebody had
already dropped the potato and everyone was just
standing around looking at it. The front office that
arrived around 2019 essentially had to rebuild the
roster from scratch using the picks that remained,
which they did successfully, which means the story has
a decent ending even if the middle chapters were
difficult reading.

21. De'Aaron Fox and Domantas Sabonis: Fast Meets Fundamentally Excellent

The modern Sacramento Kings are built around two players who have almost nothing in common stylistically and somehow make each other significantly better, which is either great roster construction or a happy accident depending on who you ask. De'Aaron Fox is the fastest guard in the league, a player whose entire identity is built around speed, attacking, and making decisions in traffic that most players cannot process standing still. Domantas Sabonis is a 6-foot-10 Lithuanian big man who does not run so much as lumber with extreme purpose, regularly putting up near triple-double numbers every season and making the Kings offense function the way a very well-organized kitchen functions. One of them is a sports car. The other is a freight train. Together they are the most effective odd couple in Sacramento basketball since Webber and Divac.

Sabonis arrived in Sacramento via trade from Indiana in February 2022 and immediately changed what the Kings were capable of. He is a passer first, a scorer second, a rebounder constantly, and a player who makes the offense easier for everyone around him because of how well he reads the game. Fox running in transition with Sabonis trailing and ready to catch is one of the harder things in the NBA to defend because you have to respect both of them simultaneously and there is simply not enough defensive coverage to go around.

The two became close off the court as well, which matters more than it sounds in professional sports. Chemistry is real. Teams that like each other tend to play harder for each other, and Sacramento under Fox and Sabonis has had a genuine culture that extends beyond the stat sheet. They are not just good players. They are the foundation of something that the Kings hope lasts long enough to finally get past the first round of the playoffs, which based on recent history is not guaranteed but is at least plausible for the first time in a long time.

22. The Analytics Era: Sacramento Finally Started Listening to the Math

For a significant portion of their history, the Sacramento Kings operated on vibes. Not exclusively, and not always to their detriment, but there were stretches of Kings management where decisions appeared to have been made by throwing darts at a list of available players while blindfolded. The results were occasionally spectacular and more often a learning experience. The franchise eventually concluded, correctly, that there had to be a better way.

The front office overhaul that began around 2019 brought in a new general manager in Monte McNair and eventually a new coaching staff, and the approach shifted toward data-driven roster construction of the kind that has become standard across the modern NBA. This means using advanced statistics to identify undervalued players, building rosters with specific skill sets that complement each other, and making decisions based on something other than a gut feeling and a highlight reel. It is less romantic than the old way. It is significantly more effective.

The results showed up quickly. The Kings assembled a roster around Fox and Sabonis that made sense positionally, played together coherently, and ended the playoff drought in 2023. The front office deserves credit for that, even if front offices are less fun to celebrate than players. Someone had to decide what pieces to acquire, what pieces to move, and what the team was supposed to look like when it was finished. Sacramento finally had people making those decisions who understood the math well enough to trust it. The math, for once, said good things back.

23. Sacramento's Growing Status as a Real NBA City

There is a version of the NBA landscape that does not take Sacramento seriously. That version is increasingly out of date. For years the Kings existed in a strange middle space, too small a market to attract free agents naturally, too passionate a fanbase to be dismissed entirely, too historically snakebitten to be considered a real destination. The city itself spent decades fighting just to keep its team, which is not the profile of a place players dream about signing with in the summer.

Golden 1 Center changed the physical argument. The 2023 playoff run changed the competitive argument. The culture around the team, the noise, the cowbells, the genuine investment of the Sacramento community in its basketball franchise, is changing the intangible argument. Players have started talking about Sacramento differently. The arena is considered one of the best in the league. The ownership group led by Vivek Ranadive has invested in the team and the surrounding area in ways that have made Sacramento a more serious place to play.

The farm to fork capital of America, a city that once had to beg the NBA to let it keep its team, is now a place where players want to come, which if you had said that out loud in 2013 during the relocation fight, people would have looked at you with extreme skepticism. Sacramento does not have the glamour of Los Angeles or the cache of New York. What it has is a fanbase that shows up with cowbells and takes every game personally, which some players genuinely prefer. Turns out authenticity is its own kind of attraction.

24. The Longest Drought Is Over: What Comes Next

The Sacramento Kings spent sixteen years without a playoff appearance. Sixteen years. To put that in perspective, a child born the last time Sacramento played playoff basketball in 2006 would have been old enough to drive, vote, and order their own food by the time the Kings came back in 2023. That is not a rough patch. That is a geological era. And yet Sacramento kept showing up, kept buying tickets, kept bringing the cowbells, and kept doing the thing that long-suffering sports fans do, which is believing with absolutely no logical basis that this year might be different.

Now the drought is broken and the question has shifted from whether Sacramento can make the playoffs to whether Sacramento can make a real run in the playoffs, which is a genuinely more interesting question and one that the Kings are actively trying to answer. The core of Fox and Sabonis is young enough to have multiple competitive windows remaining. The front office has shown it can build a coherent roster. The arena is full and loud and ready. The ingredients for something significant are present in a way they have not been since 2002, which is either exciting or terrifying depending on how much of your emotional wellbeing you have tied to a basketball team.

The Kings have not won an NBA championship since 1951, when they were the Rochester Royals and the sport barely resembled what it is today. That is a long time. That is longer than most things in modern life have existed. Sacramento fans are patient people by necessity at this point. They have been in training for this their whole lives. When it finally happens, and they genuinely believe it will, the cowbells will be audible from space.

25. The Future Is Purple and Gold

The Sacramento Kings enter their future with more reason for optimism than they have had in two decades, which if you have read this book from the beginning, you will understand is not a small statement. This is a franchise that relocated three times, nearly relocated a fourth, lost a generation of fans to the lottery, and spent the better part of the 2010s watching other teams celebrate while Sacramento rebuilt, re-rebuilt, and then rebuilt once more for good measure. That the Kings emerge from all of that with a legitimate star player, a legitimate co-star, a legitimate arena, and a legitimate front office is either a triumph of persistence or evidence that the universe eventually gets tired of being unfair. Probably both.

De'Aaron Fox is entering his prime. Domantas Sabonis is playing the best basketball of his career. Golden 1 Center is packed and loud and powered by solar energy because Sacramento is going to save the planet and win basketball games simultaneously. The cowbells are polished. Slamson is ready to be launched out of something. The farm to fork concessions are locally sourced and genuinely better than they have any right to be at a sporting event.

This is Sacramento. This is the Kings. This is the franchise that was nearly stolen, nearly abandoned, and nearly forgotten, and is now closer to something meaningful than it has been in a generation. Whatever comes next, the fans will be there. Cowbells in hand. Voices ready. Purple and gold forever.

Bonus Trivia Quiz!

You think you are a true Sacramento Kings fan? Try this bonus quiz!

1. Which city did the Sacramento Kings franchise start in before eventually moving to California?

A) Kansas City
B) Rochester
C) Cincinnati
D) Indianapolis

2. What was the name of the Kings' arena before Golden 1 Center?

A) Sleep Train Arena
B) Power Balance Pavilion
C) ARCO Arena
D) Arrowhead Pond

3. Oscar Robertson famously averaged a triple-double for an entire season. What year did he accomplish this?

A) 1959-60
B) 1961-62
C) 1963-64
D) 1965-66

4. Mitch Richmond played for Sacramento from 1991 to 1998. How many NBA All-Star selections did he earn as a King?

A) Three

B) Four

C) Five

D) Six

5. What is De'Aaron Fox's nickname?

A) Flash

B) The Fox

C) Swipa

D) Sac Daddy

6. In the 2002 Western Conference Finals Game 6, how many free throws did the Los Angeles Lakers shoot?

A) 28

B) 32

C) 36

D) 40

7. Which disgraced referee later alleged that Game 6 of the 2002 Western Conference Finals had been manipulated?

A) Joey Crawford

B) Tim Donaghy

C) Dick Bavetta

D) Steve Javie

8. In the 2013 ownership crisis, which city's ownership group tried to purchase the Kings and relocate them?

A) Las Vegas

B) Vancouver

C) Seattle

D) St. Louis

9. What was the vote count when the NBA Board of Governors decided to keep the Kings in Sacramento in 2013?

A) 17 to 13

B) 19 to 11

C) 20 to 10

D) 22 to 8

10. Golden 1 Center holds the distinction of being the first indoor arena in North America to be powered entirely by what?

A) Wind energy
B) Solar energy
C) Hydroelectric power
D) Natural gas offset credits

11. Peja Stojakovic won the NBA Three-Point Shootout at All-Star Weekend how many times?

A) Once
B) Twice
C) Three times
D) He never won it

12. What is the name of the Sacramento Kings mascot?

A) Kingsley
B) Crown
C) Slamson
D) Roary

13. Sacramento is officially known by what food-related nickname?

A) The Almond Capital of the World
B) The Farm to Fork Capital of America
C) The Golden Harvest City
D) America's Breadbasket

14. How many years passed between the Kings' last playoff appearance before 2023 and their return?

A) Twelve years
B) Fourteen years
C) Sixteen years
D) Twenty years

15. Domantas Sabonis arrived in Sacramento via trade from which team in February 2022?

A) Milwaukee Bucks
B) Indiana Pacers
C) Atlanta Hawks
D) Oklahoma City Thunder

Super Fan Secret Challenge

Only a true Sacramento Kings fan will know this.

(No Answer Provided)

Chris Webber and Vlade Divac formed one of the greatest frontcourt duos in Sacramento Kings history during the early 2000s. Name the third member of that championship-caliber starting lineup who was known for his three-point shooting and became a two-time NBA Three-Point Shootout champion.

Answer Key

1. B) Rochester

2. C) ARCO Arena

3. B) 1961-62

4. D) Six

5. C) Swipa

6. D) 40

7. B) Tim Donaghy

8. C) Seattle

9. D) 22 to 8

10. B) Solar energy

11. B) Twice

12. C) Slamson

13. B) The Farm to Fork Capital of America

14. C) Sixteen years

15. B) Indiana Pacers

NBA PLAYOFF BRACKET

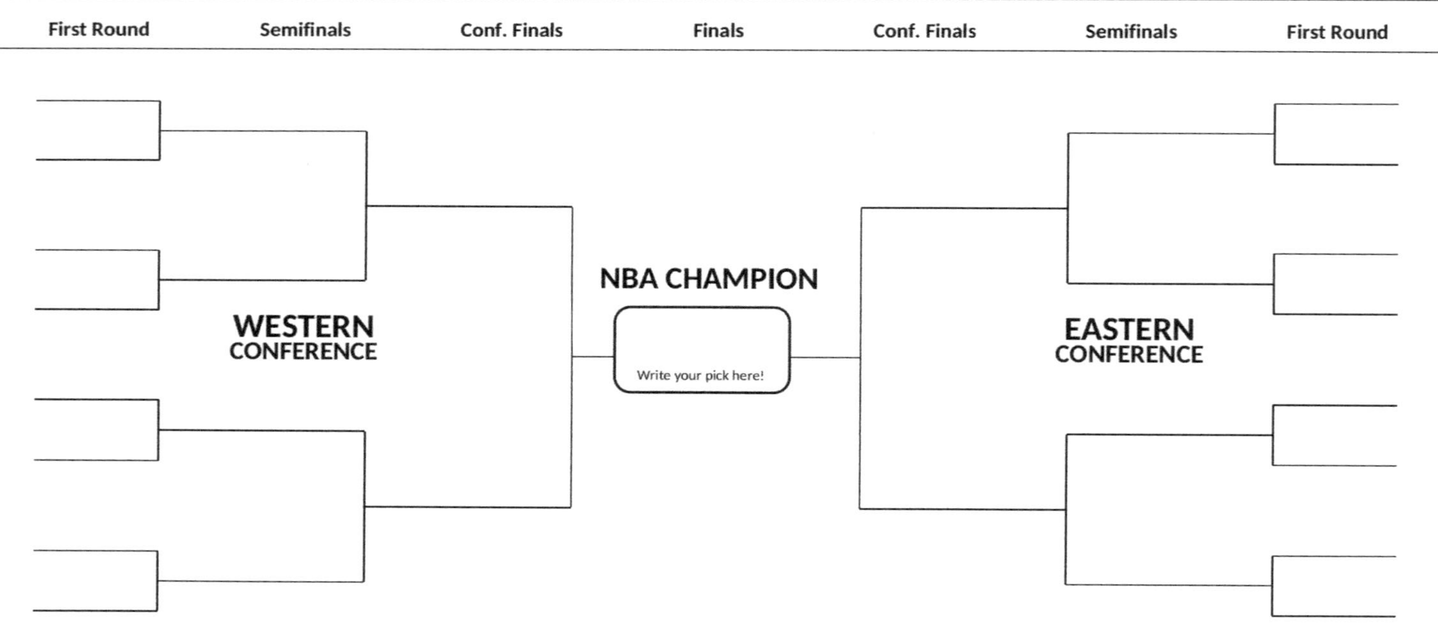

* Fill in your picks and try not to argue with your friends about it!

Part of the Fun Fan Facts: The Unofficial Sports Guide Series

Be the Boss of the Playoffs

You've broken down the matchups. You know which superstar takes over in the fourth quarter. You've seen the bench units that quietly decide series. You've watched the adjustments coaches make when their backs are against the wall.

Now it's time to stop watching and start deciding.

On this page, you are not just a fan. You are the Head Coach drawing up the last play with three seconds left on the clock. You are the GM who built this roster. You are the analyst who saw it all coming.

This is not just filling out a bracket.

This is building your championship run.

Sixteen teams enter the NBA Playoffs. The path is brutal. Best of seven. No shortcuts. No hiding. Every round gets louder, harder, and more personal.

This bracket is your Playoff Control Room.

The Game Plan

1. Survive Round One: Start with the opening round. Which matchup is going seven games? Who has the closer? Who folds under pressure? Make the calls.

2. Feel the Momentum: As you move into the Conference Semifinals and Conference Finals, things change. Role players become heroes. Stars feel the weight. Trust your reads.

3. Own the Finals: Trace your picks all the way to the NBA Finals. When the confetti falls and the trophy is raised, you'll find out who earned it.

House Rules: Circle your boldest upset. That is your official "I knew it" moment.

Choose Your Weapon: Pencil if you want flexibility. Pen if you trust your instincts. Sharpie if you believe in chaos.

Because once the playoffs tip off, there is no rewinding Game 7.

Make your picks. Trust your basketball brain. And let the playoff drama begin.

Fun Facts Wrap-Up

You made it through! You're officially a true superfan! Now it's time to put your knowledge to the test. Share these facts with friends and see who really knows their team best.

Love the series?

Your reviews help other fans discover Fun Fan Facts. If you enjoyed this book, we'd really appreciate you sharing your thoughts and leaving a review.

Want more Fun Fan Facts?

Scan the QR code below to visit our site and explore bonus trivia, challenges, and special extras - including new teams, future series, and collectible fun as they're released.

English Football Edition

☐ Arsenal F.C.

☐ Aston Villa F.C.

☐ Chelsea F.C.

☐ Everton F.C.

☐ Fulham F.C.

☐ Liverpool F.C.

☐ Manchester City

☐ Manchester United

☐ Newcastle United F.C.

☐ Tottenham Hotspur

☐ West Ham United

☐ Wrexham A.F.C.

NBA Edition

☐ Atlanta Hawks

☐ Boston Celtics

☐ Brooklyn Nets

☐ Charlotte Hornets

☐ Chicago Bulls

☐ Cleveland Cavaliers

☐ Dallas Mavericks

☐ Denver Nuggets

☐ Detroit Pistons

☐ Golden State Warriors

☐ Houston Rockets

☐ Indiana Pacers

☐ LA Clippers

☐ Los Angeles Lakers

☐ Memphis Grizzlies

☐ Miami Heat

☐ Milwaukee Bucks

☐ Minnesota Timberwolves

☐ New Orleans Pelicans

☐ New York Knicks

☐ Oklahoma City Thunder

☐ Orlando Magic

☐ Philadelphia 76ers

☐ Phoenix Suns

☐ Portland Trail Blazers

☐ Sacramento Kings

☐ San Antonio Spurs

☐ Toronto Raptors

☐ Utah Jazz

☐ Washington Wizards

About the Author

Jake is a 13-year-old sports fan who loves football, American football, and basketball. He plays soccer as a goalie and dreams of one day playing for West Ham United and helping teach kids to love the game. His passion for sports runs in the family - his dad was a professional baseball player, and his stepdad sparked his love for West Ham. Through the Fun Fan Facts series, he shares the fun and excitement of sports with fans everywhere.